Illinois History

Andrew Santella

211

Heinemann Library
Chicago, Illinois

Designed by Kimberly R. Miracle and Betsy Wernert
Printed and bound in the United States by Lake Book Manufacturing, Inc

12 11 10 09 08
10 9 8 7 6 5 4 3 2 1

New edition ISBNs: 978-1-4329-0268-1 (hardcover)
                   978-1-4329-0275-9 (paperback)

The Library of Congress has cataloged the first edition as follows:
Santella, Andrew.
  Illinois history / by Andrew Santella.
     v. cm. -- (State studies)
Includes bibliographical references and index.
Contents: Early Illinois -- Statehood -- A changing
nation -- Into the twentieth century -- A new millennium.
  ISBN 1-4034-0008-3 (HC), 1-4034-0569-7 (Pbk)
  1. Illinois--History--Juvenile literature. [1. Illinois--
History.] I. Title. II. State studies (Heinemann Library (Firm))
  F541.3 .S265 2002
  977.3--dc21
                        2002000796

Acknowledgments
The author and publishers are grateful to the following for permission to reproduce copyright material:
Cover photography reproduced with permission of CORBIS/Bettmann.

p. 4 ©Melissa Winter/Peabody Energy; **pp. 5, 12, 16, 18, 28** ©maps.com/Heinemann Library; **p. 6** ©Jonathan Blair/Corbis; **p. 7** ©Carter Sisney Photography; **p. 8** ©Courtesy of Cahokia Mounds State Historic Site; **p. 9** "Man Who Tracks, a Chief", by George Catlin. Gift of Mrs. Joseph Harrison, Jr., ©Smithsonian American Art Museum, Washington, D.C./Art Resource; **p. 10T** ©Michele Moldenhauer, Archeological Society of Virginia Artist, and the Virginia Department of Historic Resources; **p. 10B, 17T, 20T, 40B** ©Robert Lifson/Heinemann Library; **pp. 11, 13, 14B, 19B** ©North Wind Pictures; **p. 14T** ©Steve Warble; **p. 15** ©The Granger Collection, NY; **p. 17B** ©Francis Marion Pebbles (1839-1928)/Chicago Historical Society; **p. 19T** ©Henry Lewis/Wisconsin Historical Society; **p. 21B** ©Courtesy of John Deere; **pp. 20M, 21, 25, 30** ©Chicago Historical Society; **p. 21** ©Photri; **p. 22** ©Stock Montage; **pp. 23B, 24, 26T, 27, 34, 36** ©Bettmann/Corbis; **p. 23T** ©Marshall Prescott/Unicorn Stock Photos; **pp. 26B, 29T, 31, 32, 37T, 40T, 42T** ©Corbis; **p. 28** ©Illinois Department of Commerce and Community Affairs; **p. 29B** 1898 cover: Reprinted by permission of ©Sears, Roebuck and Co. Protected by copyright. No duplication permitted; **p. 33** ©Stock Montage; **p. 35** ©Edward Hattersley/Alamy; **p. 38** ©AP/Wide World Photos; **pp. 39T, 44** ©Courtesy of Fermilab; **39B** ©Scott Olson/Getty Images; **p. 41** ©U.S. Senate Historical Office; **p. 42B** ©Courtesy Ronald Reagan Library; **p. 43T** ©Alamy/Peter Ravallo; **p. 43B** ©Randy Squires/ AP photo

Every effort has been made to contact copyright holders of any material reproduced in this book. Any omissions will be rectified in subsequent printings if notice is given to the publisher.

Disclaimer

Contents

Some words are shown in bold, **like this**. You can find out what they mean by looking in the glossary.

Early Illinois

Long before people lived in Illinois, natural forces were shaping it. Millions of years ago, a watery swamp covered Illinois. Eventually, the trees and plants of the swamp died. They sank under the water and formed a kind of spongy soil called **peat**. Over many years, the weight of layers of rock and sand hardened the peat. Eventually, it turned into a black rock that is called **bituminous** coal. Today, people dig coal from the ground and burn it for heat and energy. Illinois sits atop the nation's largest supply of bituminous coal.

Long after the swamps dried up, huge glaciers stretched over Illinois. Glaciers are thick sheets of ice that do not melt as the seasons change. They can slowly spread over land, and just as slowly melt and retreat. Thousands of years ago, glaciers inched their way down from the north to cover Illinois. Four times the glaciers advanced, and four times they retreated. Each advance and retreat took tens of thousands of years.

Illinois coal mines provide over 35 million tons (32 million metric tons) of coal each year.

Illinois

Galena

Rockford

Byron

Fox River

Waukegan

Arlington Heights

Des Plaines

Elgin

Evanston

Skokie

Wheaton

Oak Park

Chicago

Dixon

Rock River

Aurora

Naperville

Mississippi River

Tampico

Rock Island

Moline

Joliet

Illinois & Michigan Canal

La Salle

Bishop Hill

Kankakee River

Kankakee

Galesburg

Illinois River

Peoria

Eureka

Pekin

Nauvoo

Normal

Bloomington

Quincy

Champaign

Urbana

Danville

Sangamon River

Springfield

Arthur

New Salem

Lake Shelbyville

Mattoon

Illinois River

Effingham

Embarras River

Godfrey

Vandalia

Alton

Edwardsville

Carlyle Lake

Collinsville

East St. Louis

Cahokia

Centralia

Mt. Vernon

Grayville

Wabash River

Prairie du Rocher

Rend Lake

Kaskaskia

Kaskaskia River

Big Muddy River

Shawneetown

Mississippi River

Carbondale

Ohio River

Cairo

N
W E
S

0   50 miles

0   50 km

The woolly mammoth (above) is an extinct relative of the modern elephant. Some mammoths were more than 14 feet (4.3 meters) tall, with tusks 13 feet (4 meters) long. Their long hair helped protect them from the severe cold of the **Ice Age**.

The glaciers helped shape the way Illinois looks today. They were so heavy that they flattened the land. They dug into the earth to create lake beds and river channels. When the glaciers melted about 12,000 years ago, the force of rushing water cut into hard rock to form beautiful cliffs. When the glaciers inched away, they left behind finely ground bits of rock. Those bits of rock were full of the minerals that make soil rich. Thousands of kinds of grasses and other plants grew in that rich soil. Much of Illinois was covered with **prairie** until the 1700s. In the 1800s, farms began to take the place of the prairie. Today that same rich soil helps make Illinois one of the nation's leading farm states.

The First Illinoisans

The first people to live in Illinois arrived about 15,000 years ago. They were wandering hunters, or **nomads**. They followed the herds of wild animals they depended on for food. These early residents of the Americas were descended from **Stone Age** people. The Stone Age people had originally come from Asia to North America across the **Bering Strait**. Over many years, groups of people moved south from what are now Alaska and Canada to settle all across North and South America.

The first Illinoisans did not live in permanent, or fixed, settlements. They made camps in forests to be near the animals they hunted. Many of the large animals they hunted are now **extinct** (no longer living), such as the **woolly mammoth** and the **mastodon**. The early Illinoisans are called Paleo-Indians, which means "ancient Indians." They hunted on foot because there were no horses in America at that time. They wrapped themselves in animal skins to keep warm in a climate that was much colder than today's.

The **Archaic period** began in about 8000 BCE. During this period, Native Americans started planting crops and harvesting them. They were Illinois's first farmers. They also gathered fruits and nuts. The people of the Archaic period invented new tools for hunting. One of the tools was called an *atlatl*. An atlatl was a wooden tool used for launching spears. A spear launched with an atlatl could travel a greater distance than one thrown by hand. This helped make people of the Archaic period better hunters.

Here is an atlatl in use. A spear launched with an atlatl could travel faster and farther than one thrown by hand. This helped people hunt large animals like the mammoth.

Monks Mound (above) is located near the present-day city of Collinsville, Illinois. It is the largest prehistoric earthwork in the United States. Visitors can still climb the mound today.

People of the Woodland culture in Illinois built villages and burial mounds. The Woodland culture lasted from about 1000 BCE to about 700 CE. Woodland people invented the bow and arrow for use in hunting. They also began making pottery. These people were part of a large trading network. They traded for seashells from the Gulf of Mexico and for copper mined near Lake Superior. They were the first to grow corn in Illinois. Anyone who has driven across Illinois recently knows that Illinoisans are still outstanding corn farmers. Illinois is one of the country's top corn producers.

This is an artist's recreation (below) of what the Mississippian city of Cahokia may have looked like in 1150 CE. Monks Mound is visible in the distance.

Around the year 900 CE, people living near the Mississippi River began building a grand city. They were part of a new culture called the Mississippian culture. The Mississippian period lasted from about 800 CE to about 1500 CE. The Mississippian city of Cahokia held as many as 20,000 people. It spread over 6 square miles (15 square kilometers) near the present-day city of Collinsville, Illinois. At the center of the city was a 100-foot (30-meter) mound that covered about 17 acres (7 hectares). The mound was probably used as a temple. It is called Monks Mound, and it still stands today. Monks Mound is the largest **prehistoric** earthwork in North America. Nearby there are about 100 smaller mounds, most of which were used as burial places.

The people of the Mississippian culture probably practiced astronomy, which is the study of the stars. They performed **sacred rituals** in large **plazas**. But by 1500, the people abandoned their cities and temples. No one is sure what exactly happened. When the first Europeans arrived in Illinois, they may have had brief contact with the people of the Mississippian culture.

Native Americans in Illinois

Not long after the decline of the Mississippian culture around 1500, a new group of people came to the area. The new people would give their name to the land they called home. They were the Native Americans of the Illinois Nation, also known as the Illinois **Confederacy**. The Illinois Nation was a group of tribes that shared a common language and defended one another against common enemies. The tribes included the Peoria, Kaskaskia, Tamaroa, Cahokia, Moingwena, and Michigamea, among others. They called themselves *Illiniwek*, which means "the men." They all spoke Algonquin, a language shared by many Native American nations of eastern North America.

This is an 1830 painting of Pah-me-cow-e-tah (Man Who Tracks), a Peoria chief. The Peoria were part of the Illinois Confederacy.

The Illinois tribes lived in longhouses (left) in the summer and wigwams (right) in the winter. Both types of house were made of wood poles covered with layers of woven mats. Longhouses were divided into rooms, with a fire pit for each family.

The Illinois tribes lived in what are now Wisconsin and Iowa and in parts of Missouri and Arkansas, in addition to Illinois. They built their villages along major rivers. In the summer, they lived in large, rectangular houses called longhouses. Longhouses were usually shared by six to ten families. The longhouses were located in the larger, more permanent villages, where the Illinois tribes farmed. In the winter, the Illinois split into smaller groups for hunting and set up smaller villages. Their winter villages had dome-shaped houses called **wigwams**. Wigwams were smaller and could be moved more easily. The Illinois grew corn and other crops. They also hunted **bison**. The Illinois worshipped a supreme being called the Master of Life. They also believed in spirits called *manitous*, which could take the form of animals or birds.

Starved Rock

Starved Rock (left) is a 125-foot (38-meter) cliff that towers over the Illinois River. According to legend, a group of Illinois was trapped atop the rock by the attack of a neighboring tribe. The Illinois were surrounded, and many starved to death there.

The Illinois were not the only Native Americans who lived in the state named for them. The Miami lived in northern Illinois, near Lake Michigan. Around 1650 Iroquois people began invading Illinois. The Iroquois were among the most feared of Native American nations. They traded with English and Dutch settlers in New York for guns. They sometimes used those guns to fight other tribes. The Iroquois knew Illinois had many beavers. Beaver **pelts** were valuable trade items. Iroquois war parties began attacking the Illinois people. In the late 1600s, other tribes moved into Illinois as well. These included the Sauk, Fox, Winnebago, Potawatomi, Kickapoo, and Shawnee.

French Explorers

Around the same time, another group of people came to Illinois territory. One day in 1673, two men walked into an Illinois tribal village near present-day Keokuk, Iowa. The two men were unlike any the Illinois had seen before. Their names were Father Jacques Marquette and Louis Jolliet. They were probably the first French people the Illinois had ever met.

After his trip through Illinois, Marquette wrote an account of the voyage. His journals help historians form a clearer picture of early French activities in the Illinois region.

French explorers found the rivers of Illinois as valuable for transportation as the native peoples had for hundreds of years.

French Exploration

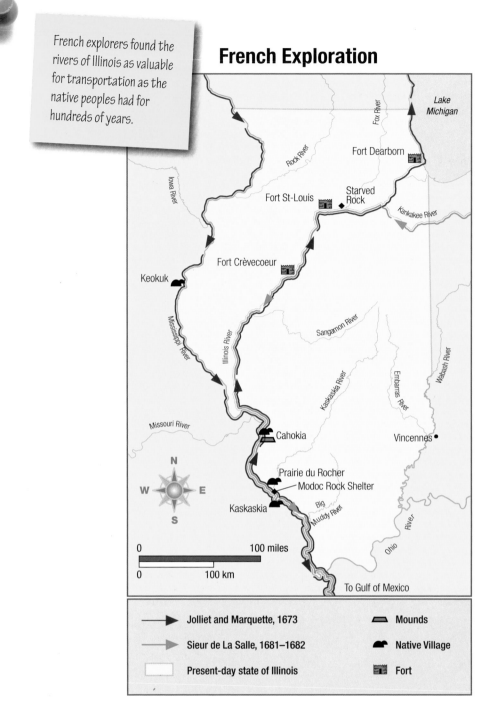

→ Jolliet and Marquette, 1673		⬯ **Mounds**
→ Sieur de La Salle, 1681–1682		⬬ **Native Village**
▢ Present-day state of Illinois		▥ **Fort**

Marquette and Jolliet were in the middle of a long journey down the Mississippi River. Their goals were to convert Native Americans they met to **Christianity** and extend France's empire in North America. They wanted to use the Mississippi River as a highway to carry furs from the middle of North America to the Great Lakes. From there they could reach French settlements in Canada and eventually make their way to Europe. Marquette and Jolliet quickly made friends with the Illinois people. The Native Americans told the explorers about a shortcut through Illinois country. Marquette and Jolliet followed the shortcut on their return trip. It took them past the place where Chicago one day would be.

Life in French Illinois

Most French villages in Illinois grew up around **Catholic** missions. Religion was the center of village life. French priests taught the children of the village and led daily religious services. The French celebrated 27 religious holidays each year. Most of the villagers were named for saints. Each person celebrated his or her saint's feast day once a year instead of his or her own birthday.

The French lived in houses made of logs stuck upright in the ground. The gaps between logs were filled with a mixture of clay and grass. A wooden porch often extended all the way around the house.

French villages included not only French people but also Native Americans and African slaves. In 1720 the first African slaves were brought to Illinois to work on French farms. The French required slaveholders to educate their slaves and **baptize** them in the Catholic religion. Slaves lived in separate houses near their owner's house. Native Americans traded with French villagers and sometimes took religion lessons from French priests. French men outnumbered French women in Illinois. Some French men married Native American women.

Children in the French villages were expected to grow up quickly. When a boy turned 12, he was considered old enough to carry a gun and defend the settlement. When a girl turned 12, she was considered old enough to marry.

La Salle failed in an attempt to return to the mouth of the Mississippi River and was murdered by members of his crew in 1687.

Another French explorer, René-Robert Cavelier, sieur de La Salle, built a **fort** along the route Marquette and Jolliet had followed. It was located near present-day Peoria. People of the Illinois Nation gathered there to trade with the French. They also looked to the French for protection. Like the Illinois, the French considered the Iroquois a threat. La Salle became friends with the Illinois and promised to protect them.

Over the next 100 years, the French built forts and cities along the rivers of Illinois. The towns of Kaskaskia and Cahokia in southern Illinois started as French trading posts or **missions**. They were to be part of a string of French **strongholds** along the Mississippi and Illinois rivers.

The French dream of an empire did not last. France was defeated in the **French and Indian War** with Great Britain, which took place from 1754 to 1763. France had to give up its North American possessions. In 1765 British troops raised the British flag over Illinois.

The American Revolution

The British had little interest in Illinois because it was far from their colonies along the Atlantic Ocean. When those colonies declared their independence in 1776, the British had very few troops in Illinois. Most of the fighting in the American Revolutionary War (1775–1783) happened far to the east. However, one important campaign brought the revolution to Illinois.

In 1778 a Virginian named George Rogers Clark led 175 volunteers to capture British forts in Illinois. Striking quickly and by surprise, Clark's troops captured Kaskaskia and surrounding towns in southern Illinois. Then Clark led his men on a daring attack on British troops at Vincennes, in what is now Indiana. His victory there meant that Illinois would one day become part of the United States.

George Rogers Clark (below) left Kentucky in 1778 to take Kaskaskia from the British. He then led a small force across rough winter terrain to capture Vincennes, Indiana.

Statehood

After the American victory in the Revolutionary War, Illinois became part of the new United States. Lands west of the Appalachian Mountains were first organized as **territories**. As the population grew, an area could apply to Congress to become a state.

In 1787 the United States government created the Northwest Territory. It included the land between the Great Lakes and Ohio River. Parts of this land would become Ohio, Indiana, Michigan, Wisconsin, Illinois, and part of Minnesota.

Settling Illinois

When the Northwest Territory was formed, the land that would become Illinois was thinly settled. In 1800 only about 2,500 people lived in Illinois. However, 12,000 new settlers entered Illinois in the next ten years. In 1809 the U.S. Congress made Illinois a separate territory. Kaskaskia became the first territorial capital.

Around the same time, a settlement was appearing on the shores of Lake Michigan. It was started by Jean-Baptiste Point Du Sable, a trader from Haiti. His trading post grew, and the area became more important as people moved west. In 1803 **Fort** Dearborn was constructed to protect the area. This settlement would one day grow into the city of Chicago.

This is what Chicago and Fort Dearborn probably looked like around 1820. With Lake Michigan and nearby rivers, this location was very valuable for trade.

Many of the people moving to Illinois traveled by riverboat. This was faster and easier than traveling by land. In 1811 the first steamboat traveled down the Ohio River, opening the way for more settlers. The new settlers built towns in southern Illinois, along the Ohio, Wabash, and Mississippi rivers. Many settlers came from Kentucky and Tennessee.

The Northwest Territory was created in 1787. Many new territories, and eventually states, came out of the Northwest Territory.

Illinois and the Northwest Territory

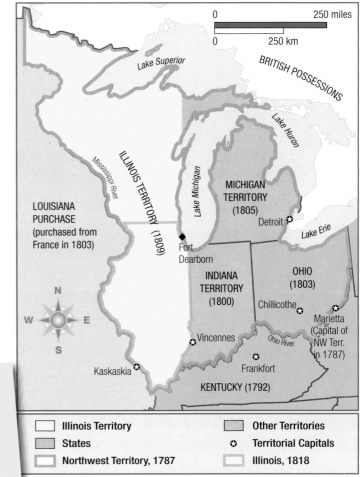

Illinois Earthquake

On December 16, 1811, the residents of the Illinois Territory received a shock. An earthquake on the New Madrid **fault** shook Illinois and the rest of the Midwest. The force of the earthquake was so strong that the course of the Mississippi River changed in several places. A large earthquake like this could happen again, but scientists think they only happen every 500 to 1,000 years on this fault.

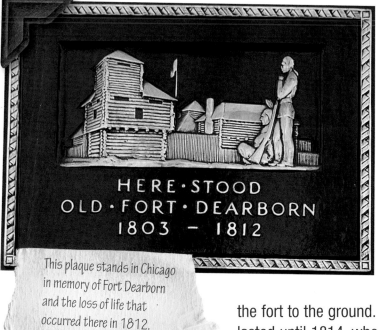

This plaque stands in Chicago in memory of Fort Dearborn and the loss of life that occurred there in 1812.

In 1812 war broke out again between the United States and Great Britain. British commanders in Canada encouraged tribes of the Great Lakes region to attack frontier settlements. On August 15, 1812, Potawatomi warriors attacked soldiers and civilians who were fleeing Fort Dearborn. They killed about 50 people and burned the fort to the ground. This war, called the War of 1812, lasted until 1814, when the United States and Great Britain signed a peace treaty in Belgium.

Becoming a State

The tragedy at Fort Dearborn discouraged some settlers, but it didn't stop Illinois's growth. By 1818 more than 34,000 people lived in Illinois. On December 3, 1818, Illinois became the 21st state in the Union. The state government rented a brick building in Kaskaskia for four dollars per day and used it as the state capitol.

If not for Nathaniel Pope (below), most of northern Illinois would now be part of Wisconsin.

Illinois gained statehood largely because of the efforts of Nathaniel Pope. Pope was Illinois's representative to the U.S. Congress. He worked with his nephew, Daniel Pope Cook, to build support for statehood. Pope also drew the map of the new state.

At first Illinois's northern border was to be just south of Lake Michigan. However, Pope recognized that the Lake Michigan shoreline would be a great advantage for a new state. Ports on the lake would help encourage trade and attract new settlers. It would also link Illinois to the other Great Lakes, which stretched all the way to the eastern United States. Pope persuaded Congress to move the northern border of Illinois about 40 miles (64 kilometers) north. If not for his efforts, most of northern Illinois would be part of Wisconsin today.

Important Waterways

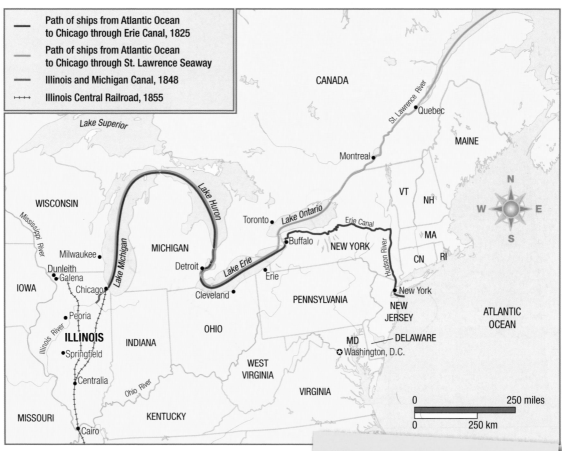

Legend:
- Path of ships from Atlantic Ocean to Chicago through Erie Canal, 1825
- Path of ships from Atlantic Ocean to Chicago through St. Lawrence Seaway
- Illinois and Michigan Canal, 1848
- Illinois Central Railroad, 1855

The new state was ideally located to receive new settlers. Settlers from the south could get to Illinois by using the Ohio and Mississippi rivers. In the north, large boats could travel to Illinois through Lake Michigan. The opening of the Erie Canal in New York in 1825 made it possible for steamboats to travel all the way from the Hudson River to Lake Michigan. Thousands of people from New York and New England traveled west over the next few decades.

The St. Lawrence Seaway opened more than 100 years after the Erie Canal, in 1959. About 50 million tons (45 million metric tons) of freight are transported on it each year.

Moving Capitals

Kaskaskia was Illinois's state capital for just two years. In 1820 Illinois moved its capital to Vandalia. Vandalia was a new city built to house the state government. It served as the capital through 1837. In 1839 voters decided the capital should be located closer to the center of the state. They voted to move the state government to Springfield, where it remains today.

This illustration shows the Battle of Bad Axe at the end of the Black Hawk War (1832). Many of Black Hawk's people were killed as they tried to cross the Mississippi River to safety.

These settlers demanded more and more land. This spelled doom for the Native Americans remaining in Illinois. As more white settlers moved into the state, they forced the Native Americans out. Most Illinois tribes moved west across the Mississippi River. The remaining Native Americans made their last stand in Illinois in 1832. That year a chief named Black Hawk led about 1,000 Sauk and Fox people into the Rock River area of northwest Illinois. They wanted to plant crops there, as they had done for centuries. However, the U.S. government sent troops to force Black Hawk and his people to move off the land. U.S. Army soldiers and Illinois volunteers chased Black Hawk's people into present-day Wisconsin. Many of Black Hawk's people were killed in the Battle of Bad Axe, as they tried to cross the Mississippi River into Iowa. The Black Hawk War ended 150 years of conflict between Native Americans and white settlers in Illinois.

Black Hawk (below) was a Sauk war chief. He took his name from the sparrow hawk, his guardian spirit.

Working the Land

Settlers moved in to work the land Native Americans had once farmed. Much of central Illinois was covered by level grasslands called **prairies**. The flat land stretched as far as the eye could see, covered by nothing but tall grass and wildflowers. Those flowers and grasses could be beautiful, but they caused trouble for farmers. Prairie plants send roots deep into the soil. Some roots might extend 15 feet (4.5 meters) beneath the surface. Farmers had difficulty cutting through the tough roots. Preparing a field for planting could be backbreaking labor.

The first settlers avoided the prairies of Illinois. But Deere's plow allowed farmers to cut cleanly through the tough roots of prairie grasses and successfully farm the whole state.

To help solve these problems, an Illinois **blacksmith** named John Deere invented a new plow in 1838. Deere's plow was made of polished steel instead of cast iron, so it sliced cleanly through the thickest roots. The steel of the plow was so smooth that soil slid right off. Deere's plow helped farmers clear the land and plant more crops.

In 1838 John Deere (above) invented a steel plow (right) that could cut through the tough roots of prairie grasses without the dirt sticking. This allowed settlers to farm the entire state of Illinois.

Life on the Farm

Early Illinois farmers faced many hardships. Many lived on lonely homesteads far from their nearest neighbors. Bad weather, sudden fires started by lightning, and diseases like **malaria** made life difficult. Only determination and hard work helped Illinois farmers make it through hard times.

Farm children were expected to do their share of the work. Farm animals had to be fed and cared for. Worn clothes and shoes had to be repaired. Without modern plumbing, even getting a drink of water was hard work. Water had to be pumped from a well, then lugged back to the house in heavy buckets. The most intense work happened during spring planting and the fall harvest. During these times, the family might work from sunrise to sundown. Children often had to miss school to help out with the farm work. In fact, many farm children only went to school some of the time and some did not attend at all. Teachers would often travel from home to home to give their lessons.

Cyrus McCormick (below) made his first reaper (left) in 1831. The reaper allowed farmers to harvest larger amounts of grain more quickly. McCormick sold his reapers all over the United States.

Cyrus McCormick's invention of the reaper also helped farmers. A reaper is a machine that helps harvest grain. McCormick made the first reaper in 1831. He then began selling them in Illinois and neighboring states. In 1847 he opened a factory in Chicago to produce reapers. It was the largest factory in Chicago at that time.

Railroads and Canals

In 1836 the state began building a canal that would link Lake Michigan and the Illinois River. The Illinois and Michigan Canal (see map on page 18) made it possible for boats to travel through the Great Lakes, to the Mississippi River, and down to the Gulf of Mexico. It helped speed up the growth of Chicago and Illinois businesses.

Not long after the canal was completed in 1848, Illinois's first railroad began operation. The Illinois Central Railroad (see map on page 18) ran from Cairo, at Illinois's southern tip, to Dunleith, in the northwest corner of the state. The first trains ran in 1855. At the time, the Illinois Central was the longest railroad in the world.

Slavery

As Illinois grew, it became divided over the issue of slavery. Since the French began settling in Illinois, people in the state had owned slaves. The Northwest Ordinance of 1787 made it illegal to bring new slaves into the territory. However, it did not free slaves already in the territory. Not until 1848, with the passage of a new state constitution, was slavery finally abolished in Illinois.

A mob murdered Elijah Lovejoy in 1837 because he had spoken out against slavery.

Many Illinoisans came from Southern states and had grown up with slavery. Others were **abolitionists**. Abolitionists were people who believed slavery was wrong and should be outlawed everywhere. An abolitionist in Alton, Illinois, named Elijah P. Lovejoy wrote newspaper articles speaking out against slavery. Angry mobs of slavery supporters destroyed his printing presses again and again. On November 7, 1837, a mob murdered Lovejoy.

The Underground Railroad

Dozens of Illinois churches, homes, and shops have been identified as Underground Railroad stops. One of the people who helped escaped slaves on the Underground Railroad was Elijah Lovejoy's brother, Owen. He hid escaped slaves in a secret space in his attic. Owen Lovejoy's house (right) still exists today. It is located in Princeton, Illinois.

Some Illinoisans fought slavery by helping slaves escape. They helped slaves flee on the **Underground Railroad**. This was not an actual railroad, nor was it under the ground. It was a route slaves followed to freedom in the North or in Canada. Escaped slaves could stop at certain locations, where they would be hidden by abolitionists.

In 1857 the argument over slavery reached the U.S. Supreme Court. The historic court case involved a slave living in Illinois named Dred Scott. Scott's owner had moved to Illinois from Missouri. In Missouri slavery was legal. In this famous 1857 case, the U.S. Supreme Court ruled that Scott remained a slave even when he left Missouri and moved into Illinois. The court also ruled that slaves were property and could not be citizens or hold any rights. The ruling angered opponents of slavery.

Dred Scott (above) was sold shortly after his famous court case. His new owner freed him, two months after the court decision.

In 1858 the argument over slavery affected the election for the U.S. Senate in Illinois. That year, a young lawyer named Abraham Lincoln ran against Stephen A. Douglas.

Lincoln believed slavery should not be allowed to spread to new states. Douglas believed new states should decide for themselves whether or not they wanted slavery. The two men debated seven times during the election campaign. Reports of the debates were printed in newspapers all over the country. They helped make Lincoln a national star. However, they did not help him win the 1858 election. Douglas became the next senator from Illinois.

Even though he lost, Lincoln's words had impressed voters. People remembered his words two years later, when he ran for president. One of his opponents in the 1860 election was Douglas. It was the first time two men from the same state competed for president. This time Lincoln won.

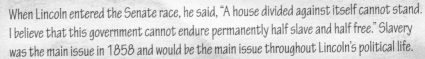

When Lincoln entered the Senate race, he said, "A house divided against itself cannot stand. I believe that this government cannot endure permanently half slave and half free." Slavery was the main issue in 1858 and would be the main issue throughout Lincoln's political life.

A Changing Nation

As president, Lincoln wanted to unite the country. But his election angered many Southerners. They feared he would try to put an end to slavery in the South. Many Southerners had vowed that their states would leave the Union if voters elected Lincoln. When Lincoln won the election, seven Southern states left the Union. On April 12, 1861, **rebels** fired on **Fort** Sumter in South Carolina. The Civil War had begun.

Lincoln's leadership helped hold the country together during the Civil War (1861–1865). Many people in Washington, D.C., made fun of Lincoln's country ways. They poked fun at his appearance and unfashionable clothes. Lincoln

had little experience as a public official, and some people wondered if he could succeed as president during a time of crisis. Lincoln proved ready for the job. His words and actions guided the American people through the crisis. In 1863 Lincoln made a speech at the dedication of a cemetery near a battlefield in Gettysburg, Pennsylvania. The speech became known as the Gettysburg Address. It explained to Americans why it was important to hold the Union together. In another speech at his second **inauguration** in 1865, he urged the North to welcome the South back into the Union after the war.

Abraham Lincoln was determined to hold the Union together. He brought the United States through its worst crisis.

Most importantly, Lincoln led the nation toward abolishing slavery. In 1863 he issued the Emancipation Proclamation. It freed all the slaves living in the Southern states that had left the Union. It was the first step toward ending the injustice of slavery. Slavery was finally outlawed in 1865 with the 13th Amendment to the U.S. Constitution. Lincoln never saw his nation reunited. On April 14, 1865, President Lincoln and his wife, Mary, attended a play called *Our American Cousin* at Ford's Theater in Washington, D.C. A man named John Wilkes Booth shot the president while he watched the play. Lincoln died the next morning. His body was returned to Springfield, Illinois, by a special funeral train. Thousands of Americans lined the railroad tracks across the nation to watch the train pass. Lincoln was buried in Springfield on May 4, 1865.

A special funeral train (above) carried President Lincoln's body back to Springfield. Thousands of people came to pay their respects as the train passed through their towns.

Grant (above) led the Union forces to victory in the Civil War. He was later elected the 18th president of the U.S.

The Civil War

Lincoln was one of many Illinoisans who gave his life for his country during the Civil War (1861–1865). Illinois sent 259,092 men to fight the war. Nearly 35,000 of them died. Illinois provided 177 of the Union Army's generals. One of these generals was Ulysses S. Grant. Grant was working in his brother's store in Galena, Illinois, when the war broke out in 1861. Since he had served as an officer in the army before, he enlisted in the war effort and was made a general. In 1864 Lincoln placed Grant in charge of all Union armies. In 1865 Grant finally forced the rebel army led by Robert E. Lee to surrender.

Grant arranged to meet Lee at Appomattox Court House in Virginia to accept his surrender. Grant brought a friend from Illinois named Ely Parker to the historic meeting. Parker was Grant's aide and a Seneca tribe member. He wrote the terms of surrender that Lee signed on April 9, 1865.

Common citizens of Illinois contributed to the war effort, too. Farmers helped feed the Union armies. Illinois women volunteered to sew uniforms and prepare bandages for hospitals. Others worked as nurses in **crude** hospitals near battlefields.

A widow from Galesburg named Mary Ann Bickerdyke saved many lives by improving hospitals. The poor conditions made it difficult for wounded men to recover. Bickerdyke worked to make hospitals cleaner and more comfortable. The Union soldiers lovingly called her "Mother Bickerdyke."

About a year after the Civil War ended, the people of one Illinois town gathered to remember their fallen soldiers. On April 29, 1866, the citizens of Carbondale met in a local cemetery for the nation's first Memorial Day. Memorial Day is now celebrated on the last Monday in May and has been a federal holiday since 1971.

Women in Uniform

Some Illinois women wanted to serve as soldiers during the Civil War (1861–1865). At the time, the army did not allow women to join. Some women disguised themselves as men and joined anyway. A Chicago woman named Frances Hook served in the army for ten months, under the name Frank Miller, before her real identity was discovered.

Bickerdyke (above) worked hard to clean up Union hospitals. She didn't hesitate to confront generals to get what she needed.

Because of its location in the United States, Illinois became a center for transportation. In fact, it had more miles of railroad track than any other state in the 1860s.

The Industrial Age

With the war over, Illinois began a period of new growth. The state's population rose quickly. In 1868 Illinois began construction on a new capitol building in Springfield to house a growing state government. The building took twenty years to complete. It is still the home of Illinois's state government. In Champaign County, the Illinois Industrial University opened in 1867. The college later became known as the University of Illinois. Today more than 30,000 students from all over the world attend classes there.

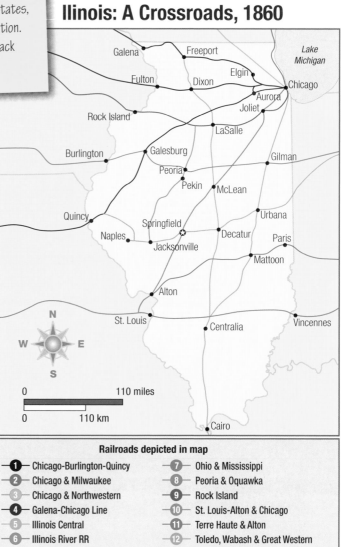

Illinois: A Crossroads, 1860

0   110 miles
0   110 km

Railroads depicted in map

1 — Chicago-Burlington-Quincy
2 — Chicago & Milwaukee
3 — Chicago & Northwestern
4 — Galena-Chicago Line
5 — Illinois Central
6 — Illinois River RR
7 — Ohio & Mississippi
8 — Peoria & Oquawka
9 — Rock Island
10 — St. Louis-Alton & Chicago
11 — Terre Haute & Alton
12 — Toledo, Wabash & Great Western

By the 1860s, railroads stretched across the country. Illinois was a crossroads for many railroad lines. It had more miles of track than any other state. Illinois became a center for transportation and **industry**.

The Illinois state capitol building (left) was completed in 1888. Its dome is actually 74 feet (22.5 meters) taller than the U.S. Capitol dome.

The Chicago Union Stockyards processed 2 million animals each year by 1870. At that time, waste from the animals flowed into the Chicago River and then into Lake Michigan.

New businesses and industries appeared all over the state. In 1865 the Union Stockyards opened in Chicago. They stood on more than 475 acres (192 hectares) of land on the city's South Side. Railroads shipped animals there from all over the country. At the stockyards, meat was prepared, packed, and shipped in refrigerated railroad cars to other cities. Chicago became a leading center for meat packaging. East St. Louis, Illinois, had its own stockyards, too.

In 1868 the Chicago Iron Company was the first to build huge blast furnaces for making steel. Companies in Joliet, Belleville, and Edwardsville also made steel. By 1880 Illinois was fourth in the nation in steel production.

Joseph F. Glidden of DeKalb developed the barbed-wire fence in 1873. The fence kept livestock out of farm fields. It became popular all over the west. Peoria became a center for liquor manufacturing. In Murphysboro, companies turned local clay into bricks. Even early baseball equipment was made in Illinois. Starting in 1876, the Spalding Company of Chicago made bats and balls.

Illinois merchants were the first to let their customers shop by mail. In 1872 Montgomery Ward began mailing his catalog to farm families who could not travel to the city to buy goods. With his catalog, they could shop for clothes and furniture without leaving home. In 1887 Sears, Roebuck and Company introduced its own catalog. Customers could even buy a complete new house from the Sears catalog.

The Sears catalog allowed people outside of cities to shop for goods they couldn't get locally.

Chicago's Growth

Chicago grew very quickly after the Civil War. However, the city was nearly destroyed by a fire that started on October 8, 1871. The cause of the fire is still unknown. It started in the cow barn at the rear of Patrick O'Leary's cottage on Chicago's West Side. Most of the city's buildings at that time were made of wood and burned easily. The flames jumped from one side of the Chicago River to the other and kept burning. When the fire finally died out, the city was in ruins. About 300 people died in the fire, and 100,000 lost their homes. Many businesses were destroyed.

Chicago did survive. **Immigrants** from all over the world came to Chicago to help build new homes and businesses. **Architects** made plans for a bigger and better city. They developed new styles and building methods. The world's first **skyscrapers** were built in Chicago. Industries thrived, and the city kept growing. By 1900 Chicago was the second-largest city in the United States.

This photograph was taken from the Chicago Water Tower after the Great Fire in 1871. The fire destroyed 18,000 buildings.

World-Class City

Chicago hosted a World's Fair in 1893. It was called the World's Columbian Exposition. The fair was supposed to mark the 400th anniversary of Christopher Columbus's voyage to America in 1492. It started a year late due to delays in planning. Twenty-seven million people from 72 countries visited the fair. It was located on grounds along Lake Michigan. People who went to the fair saw such attractions as the world's first ferris wheel (right). The exhibit buildings were designed by some of the world's top architects. The fair showed the world how Chicago had bounced back from the Great Chicago Fire of 1871.

Hard Times and Conflict

Business boomed and industry grew, but common people still struggled. The 1860s and 1870s were hard times for Illinois farmers. During the Civil War (1861–1865), farmers produced huge crops of corn to feed the Union armies. After the war, there was more corn than people needed. As a result, farmers had to accept lower prices for their corn.

In addition, large, powerful railroads often cheated small farmers. Farmers depended on the railroads to get their crops to the market. Some railroads charged very high fees to ship crops. Farmers had no choice but to pay what the railroads demanded. Farmers began organizing in order to resist unfair treatment. In 1868 they began forming local clubs called **grangers**. Grangers supported politicians who would protect small farmers.

In the late 1800s, some businesspeople made huge fortunes. At the same time, the lives of most workers remained difficult. Most people worked long hours in unsafe conditions for little pay. To fight for better pay and safer workplaces, workers formed labor unions. Labor unions are groups of workers who try to convince their employers to improve conditions or raise pay. Labor unions and business owners sometimes became enemies. Most business owners ignored the demands of labor unions. To make owners pay attention, union members sometimes went on strike. During a strike, employees protest low pay or poor conditions by refusing to work.

The Haymarket Riot (above) took place on May 4, 1886, during a time when thousands of workers across the country were occasionally on strike. It developed from a fight a day earlier between strikers and strike breakers at the McCormick Harvester plant.

Strikes often turned violent. In 1877 railroad workers in East St. Louis, Carbondale, and Peoria went on strike to protest low pay. It was called the Great Railroad Strike. In Chicago striking workers fought with police officers, and at least 18 people died.

In the 1880s, employers often made workers work very long days. Workers all over the state began demanding an eight-hour work day. On May 4, 1886, up to 3,000 workers gathered at Haymarket Square in Chicago to protest police brutality. Later that evening, police officers tried to make the last demonstrators leave. In the confusion, a bomb exploded in the middle of the crowd. Nine people were killed. Most people blamed labor unions for the violence. As a result, unions became very unpopular. However, the struggle to improve the lives of common people in Illinois went on.

Into the 20th Century

As a new century approached, more people began working for social change in Illinois. In 1889 Jane Addams began helping poor women and children in Chicago. She opened Hull House, which was a place where people in need could come for assistance. Families could find medical care there. Children attended classes. Adults could get help finding jobs. Everyone could use the library, gymnasium, and art gallery there.

Addams also worked to pass laws that would protect children. In 1883 the state passed a law that required children to attend school. In 1903 Illinois limited the number of hours children could work in factories. In 1931 Addams received the **Nobel Peace Prize** for her work. She was the second woman to win the important prize.

Jane Addams is pictured here with children at the Hull House. Residents of the house organized the first public playground and kindergarten in Chicago.

Children at Work

Employers in the 1890s and early 1900s looked for people who would work for little pay. They often turned to children. Children as young as six years old worked in the stockyards and factories of Chicago and other large cities. Their workday might last as long as 14 hours, but they were often paid less than a dollar for a day's work. Children of poor parents had to work to help their families survive. They often lived in crowded **tenements**, with few windows and little fresh air. Some poor families shared apartments with several other families.

Fighting for Rights

In 1920 the 19th Amendment to the U.S. Constitution finally gave women full voting rights. An organization called the Women's Christian Temperance Union led the campaign to give women the right to vote. The Women's Christian Temperance Union was based in Evanston, Illinois. In 1913 Illinois became the first state east of the Mississippi River to allow women to vote for president. In 1916 more than 200,000 Illinois women voted in the presidential election.

Others fought for their rights at the same time. Thousands of African Americans moved to Illinois from the south between 1910 and 1950. This became known as the Great Migration. They came looking for jobs in the many new factories. The United States entered World War I in 1917. Illinois factories expanded to produce goods for the war effort. African Americans found jobs in Illinois cities that they couldn't find in the south.

Oscar De Priest (above) was elected to the United States Congress in 1928. His father had actually been a slave.

African Americans still faced injustice in the north. In East St. Louis, white workers became angry when African Americans took jobs from striking workers. Tensions between African Americans and whites led to violence in several Illinois cities. Race **riots** broke out in Springfield and in East St. Louis. In 1919 rioting broke out in Chicago. It started on July 27, when an African-American teenager swam too close to a beach where only white people were allowed. After seven days of rioting, 38 people were dead, and many more were wounded or left homeless.

To protect their rights, African Americans began electing their own leaders. In 1928 Oscar De Priest was elected as the first African-American congressman from Illinois.

The Sanitary and Ship Canal opened in 1900, changing the flow of the Chicago River. To this day, the river is said to flow backward. Chicago's 45 movable bridges (above) let tall ships pass under and down the river.

Reforming Illinois

Illinois also took steps to make the state a healthier place. For years people in Chicago had unsafe drinking water. The Chicago River flowed into Lake Michigan. Garbage in the river polluted the drinking water in the lake. In 1900 the state completed a remarkable project to fix that problem. The Sanitary and Ship Canal opened south of Chicago. It ran 28 miles (45 kilometers) and connected the Chicago and Illinois rivers. When it was completed, the canal was the second largest in the world. Now, instead of flowing into Lake Michigan, the Chicago River flowed south into the Illinois River. As a result, Chicago was able to enjoy safer drinking water.

Illinois workplaces became cleaner and safer, too. The huge meatpacking plants in Chicago were very dirty. As a result, the meat sometimes made the people who ate it sick. In 1906 Upton Sinclair wrote about life in a meatpacking plant in the novel *The Jungle*. He showed the world just how awful conditions in these plants were. Sinclair became known as a muckraker, which is a writer who wants to expose corruption or unclean conditions. *The Jungle* created public alarm about the way meat was prepared at the plants. As a result, Congress passed laws that forbade unsafe and unclean food packaging.

Another effort to change society for the better did not work out as well. In 1919 the 18th Amendment to the Constitution outlawed the manufacture and sale of alcohol. The new law was called Prohibition. People did not stop buying alcohol. Instead they depended on criminals to supply it. Criminals formed gangs and used violence to protect their illegal business. Chicago became famous for gangsters who boldly broke the law. In three years in Chicago, 360 people lost their lives in gang violence. One of the most famous gangsters was Al Capone. Capone was finally convicted in 1931 and was sent to federal prison in 1932. Prohibition ended in 1933, with the 21st Amendment to the U.S. Constitution.

Al Capone (above) was also known as Scarface because his left cheek had a scar from a fight. He was finally convicted in 1931 for trying to avoid paying his income taxes.

The Great Depression

By 1933 Illinois and the rest of the nation were deep in the Great Depression. The Depression was one of the worst crises in the nation's history. It lasted from 1929 until about 1940. Businesses failed and banks closed. Millions of people lost their jobs and life savings. In Illinois alone, 1.5 million people lost their jobs. Coal mines shut down, and many Illinois miners were out of work. The Illinois Central Railroad fired 30,000 employees because people stopped using the railroad. Without the railroad, farmers were unable to sell their crops. In cities and on farms, many Illinoisans fell into **poverty**.

Bread lines such as this one in Chicago in 1931 were not uncommon sights during the Great Depression. Many people lost their life savings during the Depression. In Illinois, about 1.5 million people lost their jobs. Soup kitchens in cities helped provide food for the poor.

President Franklin Roosevelt tried to provide relief from the hardships of the Great Depression. He called his plan the New Deal. Roosevelt changed the way banks operated. The savings of common people would now be protected. He created new programs to put people back to work. In 1933 Roosevelt formed the Civilian Conservation Corps (CCC). The Corps worked to beautify state parks and other places. The Works Progress Administration (WPA) was formed in 1935. It built new parks, roads, and bridges. There were also artists who created beautiful **murals** in public schools and post offices.

Civilian Conservation Corps workers built the lodge (right) at Starved Rock State Park.

Helping the War Effort

Illinois civilians pitched in to help their country during World War II (1939–1945). Crops from Illinois farms fed soldiers and sailors. To produce more vegetables, more than one million people started gardens called victory gardens. They sprouted on empty lots, along railroad tracks, and even on rooftops. People also recycled scrap metal that could be used to make ammunition. The people of Peoria collected a huge pile of aluminum they named Mount Aluminum.

World War II

Illinois and the nation recovered from the Great Depression slowly. Another crisis came in 1941. The United States entered World War II (1939–1945) that year. Almost one million Illinois men and women joined the armed services. About 24,000 of them lost their lives in the war.

Illinois farms and factories worked overtime to support the war effort. The Pullman Company switched from making railroad cars to marine crafts and landing ships. The International Harvester Company stopped making farm equipment and made gun **carriages**. The Elgin Watch Company made bomb fuses. Plants in Moline, Savanna, Crab Orchard, and Kankakee supplied weapons.

Scientists in Illinois worked on a top-secret war project. They hoped to create the world's first atomic bomb. This would be the most powerful bomb ever made. Experiments that helped make the bomb possible were conducted by scientist Enrico Fermi. Fermi worked in a laboratory beneath the football grandstand at the University of Chicago. Very few people knew about his experiments, but they were important to the war effort. In 1945 the U.S. dropped an atomic bomb on each of the Japanese cities of Hiroshima and Nagasaki. The destruction was horrible, but the event helped end the war.

Many women worked in factories making weapons for World War II. These three women (below) are working on aerial torpedoes in 1943, at the International Harvester Company plant in Chicago.

The Postwar Era

During World War II (1939–1945), Illinois colleges provided training for people entering the armed services. After the war, the U.S. government helped pay for college education for **veterans**. Thousands of soldiers returned to Illinois and enrolled. Many new colleges and universities were formed after the war. Some were created by the state of Illinois.

Enrico Fermi's (above) research at the University of Chicago helped make the atomic bomb possible. The element fermium was named in his honor.

O'Hare Airport (above) was named for a World War II U.S. Naval pilot named Edward "Butch" O'Hare. O'Hare won a **Congressional Medal of Honor** for his bravery during the war.

Suburbs grew quickly as veterans bought houses. Cars became easier to afford, and people could move from cities and have more space. Suburbs also offered new schools for children.

After World War II, Illinois became an even more important transportation center. In 1955 O'Hare Airport officially opened in Chicago. The airport soon became one of the world's busiest. In 1959 the St. Lawrence Seaway opened (see map on page 18). This was a water route that ran from the Great Lakes to the Atlantic Ocean. It allowed large, ocean-going ships to sail to Illinois. This helped the economy.

Illinois's Golden Arches

In 1955 a new restaurant called McDonald's opened in Des Plaines, Illinois (left). Before long there would be thousands of McDonald's restaurants all over the world. They were the idea of a salesman from Oak Park named Ray Kroc. He went into business with the McDonald brothers of San Bernardino, California. Today McDonald's headquarters is in Oak Brook, Illinois. The company operates a school called Hamburger University, where McDonald's managers receive training.

Farm production in Illinois grew after the war. New technology and machinery made it possible to grow more crops and work more land. However, only large farms made enough money to pay for the machinery and technology. Many small farmers went out of business, and remaining farms became even larger.

Soybeans were introduced to the United States from Asia in the early 1800s. Champaign County became the leading producer of soybeans in the country. Today Illinois farmers grow about 354 million bushels (12.5 billion liters) of soybeans each year. Of course, corn remains an important crop in Illinois. McLean County in Illinois is the top corn-producing county in the nation.

Today soybeans (right) are an important crop in Illinois. They have become a popular part of people's diets. Soybeans are used in tofu, and soybean oil is used to make ink, soap, and other products.

A Century Closes

In the second half of the 20th century, Illinoisans were still fighting for equal rights for all. In the 1960s, Illinois Senator Everett Dirksen helped pass national laws that secured rights for minorities. In 1966 Martin Luther King Jr. led protests against unfair housing rules for African Americans in Chicago. King was a leader in the effort to secure civil rights for minorities in the south. To show that injustice existed in the north, too, he came to Chicago. African Americans in Chicago and other cities were denied the chance to live in some all-white neighborhoods. King marched with supporters into all-white neighborhoods to protest this injustice. His marches angered some residents and led to violence.

Violence in the Cities

In April 1968, Martin Luther King Jr. was murdered in Memphis, Tennessee. **Riots** broke out in Chicago. Nine people died and hundreds more were injured. Rioting also occurred in Carbondale, Alton, and East St. Louis. Because of this violence, many people moved away from cities. By 1970 more Americans lived in **suburbs** than in cities.

People also protested United States involvement in the Vietnam War. The Vietnam War lasted from 1957 to 1975, but most of the fighting involving U.S. troops took place from 1965 to 1969. During the Democratic National Convention of 1968, thousands of people filled the streets of downtown Chicago to protest the war. In front of television cameras, police and protesters fought on the streets of Chicago. A national television audience watched the violence in shock.

Everett Dirksen (above) helped pass the Civil Rights Act of 1964.

The 1968 Democratic Convention took place August 26 to 29. Outside the convention, thousands of anti-war protestors clashed with more than 11,000 Chicago police (above), as well as Army troops, National Guardsmen, and Secret Service.

A New Constitution

In the late 1960s, Illinoisans decided it was time for a new state constitution. The existing constitution had been passed in 1870. People believed a more up-to-date document was needed. The new constitution of 1970 aimed to protect the rights of all people. It gave women equal rights and forbade discrimination against those with disabilities.

In 1976 voters elected James Thompson governor. He was reelected three more times, making him the first Illinois governor to serve four terms. In 1980 Illinois native Ronald Reagan was elected president of the United States. Reagan was born in Tampico, Illinois, and grew up in Dixon, Illinois. He served two terms as president.

Ronald Reagan (right) grew up in Dixon, Illinois. Today, visitors can walk through his boyhood home in Dixon.

Illinois's population increased while Thompson and Reagan were in office. In 1950 Illinois was the fourth most populous state in the nation. By 1980 it was sixth. Illinois lost people and jobs to growing states in the south and southwest. In the 1980s, crop prices fell, and the value of farmland dropped. Some Illinois farmers had no choice but to sell their land and pay debts.

James R. Thompson (below) served as governor of Illinois for fourteen years, from 1977 to 1991.

Illinois **industries** went through hard times, too. Many factories closed, and workers lost their jobs. However, manufacturers remained among the state's top employers. The state also worked to encourage the growth of other kinds of businesses. Tourism in Galena, Springfield, Chicago, and other cities provided jobs in hotels, restaurants, and other businesses. New industries devoted to providing computer and other high-technology services provided more jobs. The printing and publishing industry is another one of the state's top employers.

The 21st Century

Illinois remains an important transportation center today. As more and more people travel by air, Illinois has looked for ways to handle increased air traffic. The state's population continues to grow as well. The 2000 census showed that more than 12 million people live in Illinois. That is about one million more than in 1990. It is estimated that the population in 2005 was close to 13 million.

At the same time, Illinoisans work to protect their environment. In the 1990s, cleanup efforts greatly improved the health of Illinois's rivers. This gave new hope to endangered river species like the river otter. Illinoisans also replanted and restored pieces of the tallgrass **prairie** that once covered the state.

For thousands of years, the rivers and prairies sustained the people who lived in the area. Today Illinoisans are working to give new life back to the environment. With their efforts, the people and environment of Illinois will continue to flourish well into the future.

Since 1975 volunteers have been working to restore the land around Fermilab (above) to the native tallgrass prairie that was once there.

Timeline

12,000 BCE Paleo-Indians migrate into Illinois.

8000 BCE Archaic period begins and Native Americans start planting crops.

900 CE People of the Mississippian culture build large towns and construct temple mounds.

1655 Illinois tribes clash with invading Iroquois.

1673 Louis Jolliet and Jacques Marquette are the first white men to enter Illinois.

1703 French **missionaries** found the town of Kaskaskia.

1776 The Declaration of Independence is signed.

1778 George Rogers Clark's troops capture Cahokia and Kaskaskia during the Revolutionary War (1775–1783).

1783 The Revolutionary War ends.

1787 The U.S. Congress makes Illinois part of the Northwest **Territory**.

1803 **Fort** Dearborn is built at the site of present-day Chicago.

1809 The U.S. Congress makes Illinois a territory.

1818 Illinois becomes the 21st state on December 3. Kaskaskia becomes its first capital.

1820 Vandalia becomes the capital of Illinois.

1832 Illinois settlers defeat the Sauk and Fox tribes during the Black Hawk War.

1836 Illinois builds the Illinois and Michigan Canal.

1839 Springfield becomes the capital of Illinois.

1858 Abraham Lincoln and Stephen A. Douglas debate during their campaign for the U.S. Senate.

1860 Abraham Lincoln is elected president of the United States.

1861 The Civil War (1861–1865) begins.

1871 The Chicago Fire destroys much of Chicago.

1900 The Chicago Sanitary and Ship Canal is completed.

1913 Illinois grants women the right to vote in city and presidential elections.

1929 The Great Depression begins with the crash of the stock market.

1945 World War II (1939–1945) ends and the United Nations is formed.

1964 The United States passes civil rights laws.

1968 The murder of Martin Luther King Jr. sets off **riots** in Chicago and other cities.

1970 Illinois voters approve a new state constitution.

1980 Native Illinoisan Ronald Reagan is elected president of the United States.

1986 James Thompson becomes the first Illinois governor to be elected four times.

2000 Census shows that Chicago's population grew for the first time in 50 years.

2005 The Abraham Lincoln Presidential Museum and Library opens in Springfield.

Glossary

abolitionist person calling for an end to slavery

archaeologist person who studies the remains of past human life and activities

Archaic period 8000 BCE to 1000 BCE. This is also sometimes broken up into the Early, Middle, and Late Archaic periods, and dates sometimes differ among sources.

architect person who designs buildings and gives advice on their construction

baptize purify or cleanse spiritually; baptism is a Christian ritual that uses water and receives a person into the Christian community

Bering Strait section of water that separates the continents of Asia and North America at their closest points. When Paleo-Indians first migrated to North America, the water level was lower, exposing a land bridge at this location.

bison also sometimes called a buffalo; large, shaggy-maned mammal with short horns and a hump. Bison were once plentiful in North America and were important to the native peoples for food, clothing, and shelter.

bituminous coal softer kind of coal that is dug from the ground and burned for fuel. Bituminous coal contains more carbon than some other types and has a high heating value.

blacksmith person who makes iron objects by heating them and hammering them on an anvil. Blacksmiths often make horseshoes.

carriage movable or fixed support for a gun

Catholic of the Roman Catholic faith, which is the Christian church governed by the pope in Rome

Christianity religion that came from Jesus Christ and is based on the Bible; Eastern, Roman Catholic, and Protestant churches are Christian

confederacy two or more groups that pledge to act together, especially for defense against attack

Congressional Medal of Honor military decoration awarded by the U.S. Congress for exceptional bravery at the risk of life in combat with an enemy

crude rough; not carefully made

extinct no longer living

fault fracture in the Earth's crust

fort strong building used for defense against enemy attack

French and Indian War war that took place in America from 1754 to 1763 between the French and their Native American friends on one side, and the British and their Native American friends on the other

granger national organization that works to help farmers

Ice Age period of time when a large part of the Earth was covered with glaciers and the temperatures were cooler

immigrant person who comes into a foreign country to make a new home

inauguration public and formal ceremony of placing a person in office

industry kind of business

malaria disease caused by mosquito bites resulting in fever and chills

mastodon large, extinct animal, similar to an elephant, with tusks and shaggy hair

mission place where missionaries live and work; a missionary is a person sent by a church to spread its religion

mural large picture that is painted or put on a wall

Nobel Peace Prize yearly prize given to those who work for the interests of peace and humanity

nomad person who doesn't live in any one location, but moves around to be close to a supply of food

peat soft material in the ground formed when grass and plants die

pelt skin taken from an animal

plaza public square in a city or town

poverty condition of being poor

prairie large area of flat land with a lot of grass and very few trees

prehistoric from the time before history was written

rebel soldier who fought for the Confederacy (Southern states in rebellion) in the Civil War

riot great disorder, confusion, or violence by a crowd of people; to take part in a riot

sacred ritual important and honored form or system of actions, especially in a religion

skyscraper very tall building

Stone Age first known time in which people used stone tools; of this time

stronghold fort or other place controlled by a group of people

suburb city or town just outside a larger city

tenement old, crowded apartment in the poor part of a city

territory area of land in the United States that is not organized as a state but has its own local government

Underground Railroad system in the United States in which people who were against slavery secretly helped escaped slaves reach the North or Canada

veteran person who has served in the armed forces during a war

wigwam dome-shaped Native American hut with a frame of poles covered with bark, rush mats, or animal hides

woolly mammoth large, extinct animal, similar to an elephant, with shaggy hair and long tusks that curve upward

Find Out More

Further Reading

Anderson, Kathy P. *Illinois.* Minneapolis, MN: Lerner, 2004.

Burgan Michael, Jean F. *The Lincoln-Douglas Debates*. Minneapolis, MN: Compass Point, 2006.

Marx, Christy. *The Great Chicago Fire of 1871*. New York: Rosen, 2004.

Sievert, Terri. *Illinois*. Mankato, MN: Capstone, 2003.

Websites

http://www.historyillinois.org/hist.html
This Illinois history resource page provides links to many sites about the people of Illinois, as well as the state's government, history, and symbols.

http://www.illinois.gov/facts/history.cfm
This Illinois government-run site features amazing historical facts about the state. It covers 1673 to the present.

Index